ANNE FRANK

ANNE FRANK

OUT OF THE SHADOWS

ANNA LEIGH

LERNER PUBLICATIONS ◆ MINNEAPOLIS

Lerner Publications Company
An imprint of Lerner Publishing Group, Inc.
241 First Avenue North
Minneapolis, MN 55401 USA

For reading levels and more information, look up this title at www.lernerbooks.com.

Image credits: Studio Delia/Anne Frank House, p. 2; Anne Frank House, Amsterdam. No known copyright restrictions, pp. 6, 9, 10, 11, 15, 18, 19, 33, 35, 38, 39, 40, 41; Galerie Bilderwelt/ Getty Images, p. 8; ullstein bild Dtl./Getty Images, pp. 12, 21; Universal History Archive/Getty Images, p. 13; New York Times Co./Getty Images, p. 14; Roger Viollet/Getty Images, p. 16; Album/Alamy Stock Photo, p. 17; The Granger Collection, New York, p. 20; AFP/Getty Images, p. 22; robertharding/Alamy Stock Photo, p. 23; Heritage Images/Getty Images, p. 25; dpa picture alliance/Alamy Stock Photo, p. 27; Hulton Deutsch/Getty Images, p. 29; Mondadori Portfolio/ Getty Images, p. 30; Galerie Bilderwelt/Getty Images, p. 32; Bettmann/Getty Images, p. 34; Archive Photos/Stringer/Getty Images, p. 37.

Cover Image: ullstein bild Dtl./Getty Images.

Main body text set in Rotis Serif Std 55 Regular 13.5/17. Typeface provided by Adobe Systems.

Library of Congress Cataloging-in-Publication Data

Names: Leigh, Anna, author.
Title: Anne Frank : out of the shadows / Anna Leigh.
Description: Minneapolis, MN : Lerner Publications, [2019] | Series: Gateway biographies |
    Ages 9–14 ; Grades 4–6. | Includes bibliographical references and index.
Identifiers: LCCN 2018060927 (print) | LCCN 2019000305 (ebook) | ISBN 9781541556805
    (eb pdf) | ISBN 9781541539174 (lb : alk. paper) | ISBN 9781541574304 (pb : alk. paper)
Subjects: LCSH: Frank, Anne, 1929–1945—Juvenile literature. | Jewish children in the
    Holocaust—Netherlands—Amsterdam—Biography—Juvenile literature. | Holocaust, Jewish
    (1939–1945)—Netherlands—Amsterdam—Juvenile literature. | Amsterdam (Netherlands)—
    Biography—Juvenile literature.
Classification: LCC DS135.N6 (ebook) | LCC DS135.N6 F73397 2019 (print) | DDC 940.53/18092
    [B] —dc23

LC record available at https://lccn.loc.gov/2018060927

Manufactured in the United States of America
1-45100-35927-4/2/2019

CONTENTS

German-Born   11

The Annex   15

Life in Hiding   18

Fear and Tension   21

The Diary   24

Found   28

Anne's Legacy   33

Education and Understanding   36

Important Dates   42
Source Notes   44
Selected Bibliography   45
Further Reading   46
Index   48

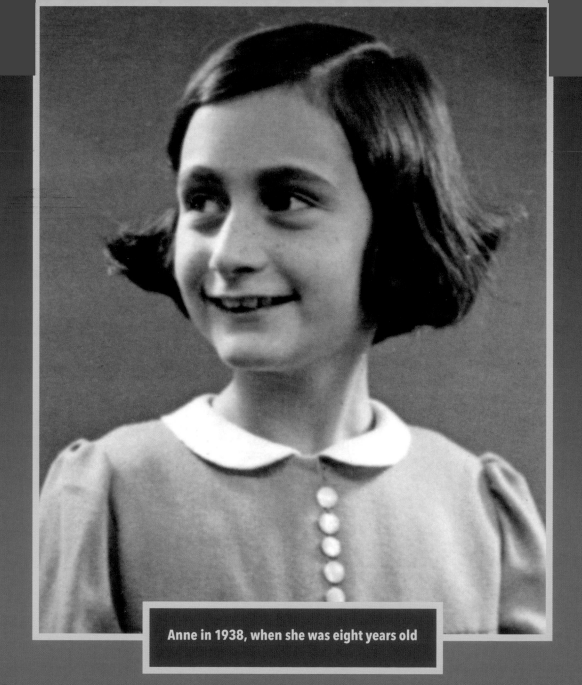

Anne in 1938, when she was eight years old

At three in the afternoon on July 5, 1942, a doorbell rang at 37 Merwedeplein, an apartment building in Amsterdam in the Netherlands. Thirteen-year-old Anne Frank was upstairs on the balcony, reading in the sunshine. She didn't hear the doorbell, but her mother and older sister, Margot, did.

At the door was a postal worker with a letter for Margot, who was sixteen years old. The letter was an official document from the German military calling her to report to a train station. From there, a train would take her to Germany. Though it was summer, the letter told her to pack a suitcase with winter clothes.

Anne's family was Jewish, and they lived in an area of Amsterdam where many other Jewish families lived. Two years earlier, the German army had invaded the Netherlands and enacted laws to restrict and hurt Jewish families. Anne and Margot had to leave their public school to attend an all-Jewish school. They could no longer visit public movie theaters or swimming pools. They couldn't ride streetcars or own bicycles. They had to wear a yellow star on their clothing that identified them as Jews.

Anne and Margot knew what the letter meant. The German military had begun removing Jews from their homes, taking their belongings, and banning them from their jobs. Many were sent to camps known as labor camps or concentration camps. At these camps, some Jews were forced to do hard labor for the Germans. Others were killed immediately. No one in Amsterdam knew exactly what the camps were, but they had heard rumors that the conditions were terrible. They feared the letters demanding they report to the camps.

Nazis forced Jewish people to wear badges like this one.

A few days before Margot received the letter, Margot and Anne's father had told Anne that the family planned to go into hiding. They would hide so the Germans could not send them to the camps. When Margot received the letter, Anne knew that it was time for the family to put the plan into action. Anne and Margot began packing their most valued belongings. Anne put books, a comb, old letters, and her brand-new diary into a bag.

Later that night, some family friends came to the Frank apartment. They hid bundles of clothing and shoes under baggy rain jackets and brought the bundles somewhere secret. The next morning, it was pouring rain. This was good—it meant there wouldn't be too many soldiers around. Anne's mother woke her at five thirty in the morning. Anne dressed in several

Anne at her school desk in 1940

layers of clothing. Margot got on a bicycle and rode away first. At seven thirty, Anne and her parents also left their home. Her parents left a note with an address on a desk. If anyone read it, they would think the family had fled to Switzerland. Anne said only one goodbye: to her cat, Moortje. She had no idea where they were going.

As Anne walked down the street with her parents, they began to reveal the plan to her. A year earlier, Anne's father had begun making plans to move the

Anne with her older sister, Margot (*left*), in 1933

family into hiding. He had told a few trusted friends about the plan. These friends and Anne's parents had been collecting clothing, canned food, and furniture ever since. They had set up a secret apartment and planned to move there on July 16. However, because of the letter Margot had received, they were moving ten days early. The apartment was not completely ready yet.

Finally, Anne learned that they were going to her father's office building at 263 Prinsengracht. The building was on a canal, which is common in the Netherlands. Only a few people worked in the office, and several of them had agreed to help the Frank family hide. The office building was tall and narrow. The Frank family would be moving into the back part of the third and fourth floors. They had a small living room, a few bedrooms, a bathroom, and a kitchen. They planned to live there until the Germans left and they were safe again.

Two days after the family moved into their hiding place, Anne wrote about it in her diary, which she had nicknamed Kitty. Nicknaming her diary made Anne feel as if she were writing to a best friend whenever she wrote her diary entries. "So much has happened it's as if the whole world had suddenly turned upside down," she wrote. "But as you can see, Kitty, I'm still alive, and that's the main thing."

GERMAN-BORN

Anne's family was originally from Germany. Her father, Otto Frank, was born in Frankfurt, Germany, on May 12, 1889. His family owned a bank. At the age of nineteen, Frank went to New York to learn about banking and business. He returned to Germany in 1909 after his father's death to work in the family bank.

The Frank family in 1941

Soon after, World War I (1914–1918) broke out. Frank joined the army and fought for Germany in the war. In 1925 he married Edith Hollander. The couple settled in Frankfurt, and Frank continued working for the bank. Their first

Adolf Hitler

daughter, Margot Betti, was born on February 16, 1926. Anne—whose full name was Annelies Marie—was born on June 12, 1929.

After Germany lost World War I, life there began to change. The country was in a financial crisis, and the Frank family bank began to lose money. Meanwhile, many people in Germany began to harbor anti-Semitism, or prejudice against Jews. They wrongly believed that Jewish people were responsible for Germany's defeat in the war and the financial struggles the country faced.

In January 1933, the German president gave Adolf Hitler a prominent position in German politics. Hitler had a long history of anti-Semitism. He was the leader of the Nazi political party, which gained a lot of power after World War I. Hitler soon became a dictator. He had complete control of the German government. In April the government began to enforce a boycott of Jewish products and services. This meant that non-Jewish Germans were discouraged from shopping in Jewish-owned stores, for example, or from visiting Jewish doctors or dentists.

Frank decided it would be safest for his family to leave Germany. He was able to get a job as the manager of a business called Opekta-Werke in Amsterdam. The company sold spices and a substance used in making jam. Frank moved to Amsterdam in 1933. His family joined him a year later.

For a while, the family led a happy life in Amsterdam. The jam and spice business was growing. Margot and Anne both attended public school. Margot was quiet and did very well in her classes. Anne was a friendly, happy, popular girl who had many friends and loved to talk and laugh. She loved being the center of attention and acted in plays at school. Her favorite thing was to try to make others laugh.

Then, in 1939, World War II (1939–1945) broke out when Germany invaded Poland. In 1940 Germany invaded the Netherlands as well and placed Dutch citizens

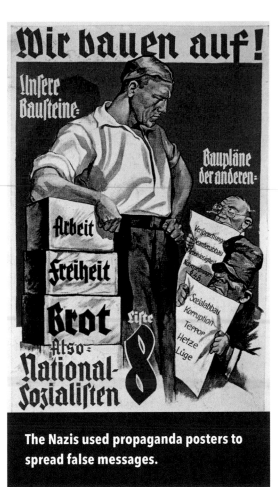

The Nazis used propaganda posters to spread false messages.

Nazi troops hold anti-Semitic posters.

under German law. The Germans enforced anti-Jewish laws in the Netherlands just as they did in Germany. They froze Jewish bank accounts so that Jewish people could not use or access their own money. The Germans allowed Jews to go to certain shops only at certain times, and they weren't allowed to leave their homes at night.

As the rules against Jews became stricter, Frank began to make plans for his family's safety. He tried to find a way to move his family away from Europe. He applied for paperwork that would allow them to move to the United States or Cuba. He wrote to his friends and relatives in the United States to ask them for help. However, by 1939, three hundred thousand Germans were already on waiting lists to enter the United States. Germany was making it harder for them to leave the country. Meanwhile, the United States was growing wary of bringing in so many new people. When the United States entered the war in 1941, President Franklin D. Roosevelt halted most immigration. Frank decided it was unlikely his family would be able to leave Amsterdam. He secretly began to prepare their hiding place instead.

THE ANNEX

On June 12, 1942, just before her family went into hiding, Anne received a red-and-white checked diary for her birthday. She began writing in it immediately. In her first entry, she wrote, "I hope I will be able to confide everything to you, as I have never been able to confide in anyone, and I hope you will be a great source of comfort and support."

Anne diligently recorded thoughts about her birthday party, her friends, and her school. She also wrote about the war, recording the things that had been taken from Jews. Anne was frustrated by the injustices Jewish people faced.

On July 8, 1942, Anne began writing in her diary from her family's hiding place. She wrote of what had happened

The red-and-white checked diary Anne received for her thirteenth birthday

when Margot received the concentration camp letter and about her family going into hiding. Anne described the office building at 263 Prinsengracht and the rooms in her family's hiding place. She called it *Het Achterhuis*, or the Annex.

When they arrived in the hiding place, Anne and her father set to work trying to make it a comfortable home for the family. Because they had moved in earlier than planned, the hiding place was filled with unorganized furniture and canned food. Anne's mother and Margot were too shocked and terrified to help, so Anne and her father unpacked boxes and cleaned the space. They hung curtains and made the beds. Anne was allowed to hang pictures on her bedroom wall of movie stars she cut from magazines. She and Margot shared one room, and their parents shared another.

On July 13, another Jewish family moved into

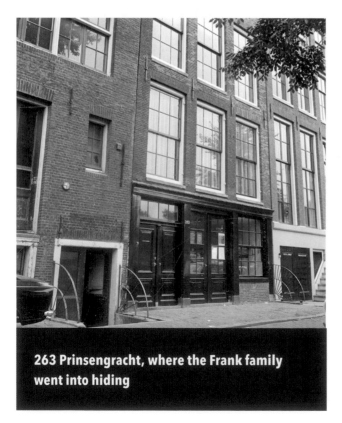

263 Prinsengracht, where the Frank family went into hiding

the hiding place with the Frank family. They were Hermann and Auguste van Pels and their son, Peter. Peter was the same age as Margot. Hermann van Pels had worked as a spice expert for Opekta-Werke, and he and Otto Frank had planned the hiding place together. The van Pels family moved into the second floor of the building. The van Pels slept in the room that also served as the main living space and kitchen for everyone in hiding. Peter had a tiny room of his own under the stairs that led to the attic of the building.

Peter van Pels

Nobody knew how long the war would last. They would not be able to leave the hiding place for any reason until the Germans left Amsterdam. Several Opekta employees—Miep Gies, Bep Voskuijl, Johannes Kleiman, and Victor Kugler—agreed to help by secretly buying groceries and other necessary items for those in hiding. The four helpers visited the hiding place each day to bring

Miep Gies

the Frank and van Pels families news of Amsterdam and the war. They also brought new clothing and shoes when they could.

It was very dangerous to help Jews in hiding. The Germans had made it illegal to help a Jewish person. If anyone had found out about the hiding place, the Franks, van Pels, and their helpers would have been arrested and sent to concentration camps or killed.

But at that time in the Netherlands, many people were working against the Germans. They were the Resistance. More than twenty thousand Dutch citizens helped hide Jewish people. Others worked secretly to pass information about the war or to get extra food or medicine for those in hiding. These Dutch citizens felt that it was worth the risk to help others. They did not want to give in to the German soldiers who had taken over their lives.

LIFE IN HIDING

At the end of 1942, an eighth person, Fritz Pfeffer, moved into the hiding place. He was Miep Gies's dentist in Amsterdam. Pfeffer was Jewish, and Gies was not. Under German rule, Gies was not supposed to visit Pfeffer, but she continued to do so anyway. In November, during a checkup, Pfeffer quietly asked Gies if she knew of a hiding place.

Pfeffer had also been a friend of Otto Frank before the war. When Gies told Frank about her conversation with Pfeffer, Frank spoke with the others in the hiding place. Together, they decided that there was room for one more. A few days later, Pfeffer moved in. He shared a room with Anne, and Margot moved into their parents' room.

Fritz Pfeffer

The hiding place was very small for eight people to live in. They all worked together to create a routine for their life in hiding. Everyone helped cook and clean. They ate meals together, and they had a schedule for when to sleep, wake up, use the bathroom, and take baths.

The Opekta business was still running below them, so workers were in the warehouse and office each day. Most of these workers had no idea that eight people were hiding in the building. It could have been very

This room served as both a living room and a kitchen in the hiding place.

dangerous if the workers discovered them. To avoid raising suspicion, those in hiding had to be very quiet throughout the day. They didn't cook or flush the toilet. They wore socks and no shoes to muffle their footsteps.

Each evening when the workers left for the day, Gies or one of the other helpers would come upstairs to tell them that it was safe to move around and speak normally. The helpers would bring groceries and discuss the latest news. At night Anne and the others would listen to the radio together. The radio and their visits with Gies, Kugler, Kleiman, and Voskuijl were their only connections to the outside world.

FEAR AND TENSION

As time wore on, tensions grew among those in hiding. Anne was chatty, and she liked to be involved in conversations with the adults. But she felt that the

Anne and Pfeffer's room in the hiding place

War planes often flew overhead, frightening those in hiding.

others in the hiding place treated her like a child. Anne especially had tensions with Auguste van Pels and Pfeffer. They scolded her for talking too much and accused her of acting like a spoiled child. Anne thought that they were too opinionated and proud.

Other tensions grew as well. The families had to be careful about how they spent their money and used up supplies. Arguments developed about what items to share and about how to divide food and cook meals. They also lived in constant fear of discovery. Opekta-Werke was robbed more than once while the families were in hiding, and unexpected visitors such as carpenters and plumbers sometimes came to the office. To help with security, Voskuijl's father built a bookcase in front of the door to the hiding place. Those in hiding could latch the door from the inside.

Anne felt most afraid at night. When it got quiet, she could hear every sound in the building. Planes often flew overhead, and she could hear bombs and gunshots in the distance. One evening in November 1943, Anne wrote, "Miep often says she envies us because we have such peace and quiet here. That may be true, but she's obviously not thinking about our fear."

Miep Gies, however, learned about their fear. Anne loved it when Gies or the other helpers would visit the hiding place. She began to ask whether Gies might stay overnight in the hiding place. One night, Gies and her husband, Jan Gies,

The attic of the hiding place, where Anne liked to sit and write

agreed to stay. Miep Gies found that she could hear every sound in the building. A nearby church clock chimed every fifteen minutes, and she thought it sounded much louder than it did during the day. She didn't sleep that night. "The quietness of that place was overwhelming," she later said. "The fright of these people who were locked up here was so thick I could feel it pressing down on me."

Despite their fear and tensions, however, the families tried to make the best of their situation. Anne and Peter spent time together, developing a friendship and eventually feelings for each other. The families made sure to celebrate each person's birthday as well as Hanukkah and St. Nicholas' Day, a Dutch holiday in December. They wrote funny poems and got small gifts that Miep Gies and Voskuijl could purchase for them. Sometimes they were able to save up for cakes or other special food. As the war went on, it became more and more difficult to get any food at all. They might have only a few potatoes or eat only beans or spinach for a time. It was a big treat to have extra food or sweets.

THE DIARY

To remain occupied during their long days and nights in hiding, Anne and the others read books and studied. Gies and Voskuijl signed up for courses that were sent by mail. Then Margot, Anne, and Peter would complete the lessons. They all studied Dutch, French, and Greek. Anne became interested in

Anne pasted photographs into her diary too.

history, mythology, and genealogies, or family trees.

Along with studying and reading books, Anne spent a lot of time writing in her diary. She wrote about their daily routines and the war. She wrote a lot about the food they were eating and the books she read.

Anne also wrote down conversations that happened in the hiding place. She recorded how everyone felt about the war and what each person dreamed of doing when it was over. They longed for hot baths, good coffee, cake, and the freedom to move around and go outside.

Anne couldn't wait to return to school. She longed to have fun and be with her friends. She wanted to be outside and feel fresh air again. She began spending time in the attic, sitting near a window. She loved being able to catch glimpses of the outside world and to watch the sky and the clouds.

Anne also wrote about her dreams for the future beyond the end of the war. She hoped that one day she might become a journalist or an author. She thought she might live in France or England, and she longed to do something worthwhile with her life. "I want to be useful or bring enjoyment to all people, even those I've never met," she wrote. "I want to go on living even after my death!"

HOPE IN HIDING

Anne thought about religion often while in hiding. After all, the Nazis were persecuting the Jews based on their religion. She often felt despair about the war. "I simply can't imagine the world will ever be normal again," she wrote in November 1943. However, she also had hope. She trusted that God would protect the Jewish people. She also believed that the war would end and that there would be goodness in the world again. In July 1944, she wrote, "I feel the suffering of millions. And yet, when I look up at the sky, I somehow feel that everything will change for the better, that this cruelty too will end, that peace and tranquility will return once more."

Along with her diary, Anne began writing essays and short stories. She thought she was a good writer, but she sometimes had doubts about her talent. "When I write I can shake off all my cares," she wrote. "My sorrow disappears, my spirits are revived! But, and that's a big question, will I ever be able to write something great, will I ever become a journalist or a writer?"

In 1944, while Anne was listening to a radio broadcast from a Dutch politician, she learned that once the war was over, the politician wanted to collect letters and diaries that Dutch people had written about their

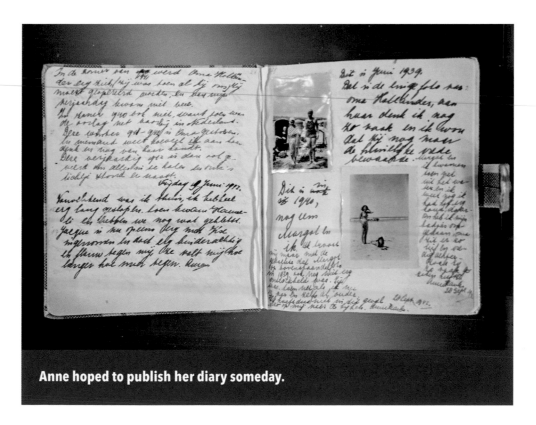

Anne hoped to publish her diary someday.

experiences. Anne immediately thought of her own diary. "Just imagine how interesting it would be if I were to publish a novel about the Secret Annex . . . ten years after the war people would find it very amusing to read how we lived, what we ate and what we talked about as Jews in hiding," she wrote.

Anne began reading back through her diary. She edited it and rewrote sections with the idea that it might be published someday. She knew she should protect the identities of those involved in the story, so she changed their names. She also cut out sections that she didn't want the world to see and rewrote others so they were more interesting.

FOUND

On Friday, August 4, 1944, Miep Gies was working in the office when suddenly she looked up to see a man standing in the doorway holding a gun. A car with several Nazi soldiers and police officers pulled up. Someone had told them that there were Jews hiding at 263 Prinsengracht. The men walked into the building and went straight up the stairs to the hiding place. They arrested Kugler, Kleiman, and everyone in hiding. They raided the rooms to take anything of value. However, they had mercy on Gies and did not arrest her.

Kugler and Kleiman were sent to prison in Amsterdam and then a work camp a month later. Soon Kleiman was

An electric fence separates men and women prisoners at a German concentration camp.

released because of his poor health. Kugler escaped in March 1945 as he was being taken to Germany.

Anne and the others from the hiding place were sent to Westerbork, a holding place for Dutch Jews before they were shipped to other camps. In September 1944, all eight were brought by train to Auschwitz, a concentration camp in Poland.

Soon after they arrived at Auschwitz, Hermann van Pels was killed by poisonous gas. Later, Auguste van Pels was sent to another camp, Theresienstadt, in modern-day Czech Republic. Margot and Anne were considered strong enough to go to Bergen-Belsen, a work camp in northern Germany. Peter van Pels was forced to march from Auschwitz with a group of other prisoners to Mauthausen, in Austria. Meanwhile, Fritz Pfeffer was moved to Neuengamme, in Germany. He died in December 1944. Peter and Auguste van Pels both died in 1945. Edith Frank died at Auschwitz of starvation in January 1945. Anne and Margot both died of typhus, a disease carried by lice, at Bergen-Belsen in February 1945. Anne was just fifteen years old. Otto Frank was the only one of the group to survive the war. On January 27, 1945, Soviet forces arrived at Auschwitz to liberate it from German control. Frank was free.

The entrance gate at Auschwitz, where Anne was separated from her parents

THE HOLOCAUST

The persecution of Jews during World War II is known as the Holocaust. Hitler and his supporters planned to kill all nine million Jews who were living in Europe. The persecution began in Germany. By 1939 more than half of the Jews in Germany had moved to other countries in Europe. On September 1, 1939, Germany invaded Poland, which had a large Jewish population. During World War II, Germany invaded other European countries, including France and the Netherlands. In each country, Nazis rounded up Jews and took them from their homes. Groups of Jewish people were shot, killed by poisonous gas, or made to live in terrible conditions where they would die of disease or starvation. The Nazis also killed millions of others, including people with disabilities, Roma people, and gay people.

World War II in Europe ended in May 1945. By then six million Jews had been killed. In the Netherlands, more than one hundred thousand Jews were sent to camps. Just fifty-two hundred survived. Another twenty-five thousand to thirty thousand Jews went into hiding in the Netherlands. About two-thirds of these people survived.

Survivors of Auschwitz leaving the camp at the end of World War II

In June 1945, Frank returned to Amsterdam. He reunited with Miep Gies and lived with her and her husband. He also returned to work at Opekta. He knew that his wife had died in Auschwitz. He did not know, however, what had happened to Anne and Margot. He hoped they were still alive. For weeks, he wrote letters asking people he knew if they had heard news of Anne and Margot.

One day, Frank learned from someone who had been at Bergen-Belsen that Anne and Margot had both died. He shut himself in his office to mourn privately. A few hours later, Gies approached him holding a stack of papers. Following the arrest, she and Voskuijl had gone up to the hiding place. They noticed the pages of Anne's diary strewn around the rooms and quickly gathered them up. Gies was afraid the soldiers would come back and take everything from the hiding place. She kept the diary in her desk drawer so she could give it back to Anne after the war. Instead, she gave the pages to Frank. "Here is your daughter Anne's legacy," Gies told him.

ANNE'S LEGACY

Frank read the words Anne had written. As he mourned the loss of his family, he remembered his daughter and experienced her personality again through her words. He learned what she had thought of those in hiding. He read about her hopes and dreams. He understood what she had known and perceived about the war raging in Europe. He was impressed by her writing, intelligence, and imagination.

Otto Frank

READING THE DIARY

Though Miep Gies took Anne's diary from the hiding place after the arrest, she did not read it until many years later, when it was published. Otto Frank encouraged Gies to read it several times, but she always refused. She did not want to relive the pain of that time. When Gies finally agreed to read the diary, she read it in one sitting. She realized it was a good thing she had not read the diary when she first found it, as she would have burned it to protect those Anne had written about. She also found that she did not experience the pain she had expected. Instead, she was glad to read Anne's words. "So much had been lost," she later wrote, "but now Anne's voice would never be lost. My young friend had left a remarkable legacy to the world."

Miep Gies in 1987

As he read, Frank felt a desire to share Anne's words with others. He translated parts of the diary and sent them in letters to his mother in Switzerland. Eventually, a friend of his found out about the diary and asked to read it. He thought the diary was an important account of the war and encouraged Frank to publish it. Frank resisted at first but later agreed. He edited the book and removed sections that he thought were too personal or private. Though the war was over, he kept the nicknames Anne had given the characters in the diary. He wanted to keep protecting the identities of those who had been involved.

Het Achterhuis, the first publication of Anne's diary, in 1947

On June 25, 1947, Anne's diary was published in the Netherlands. The title of the book was, as Anne had intended, *Het Achterhuis*. A few years later, in 1950, the book was translated and published in Germany and France. In 1952 the diary was translated into English, published in the United States, and titled *The Diary of a Young Girl*. It became an instant best seller. Since then the diary has been translated into more than seventy languages. Some historians say that the diary is one of the most well-read documents of World War II.

AN AUTHENTIC TEXT

There are several versions of Anne's diary. Anne wrote the original version of her diary before and during her time in hiding. After 1944 she began editing her diary in the hopes that it would be published one day, creating the second version. Otto Frank created a third version when he edited his daughter's words for publication. This version mixes pieces of Anne's original and her revisions. In 1997 a complete version of the diary was published that includes the pieces that Frank's version left out. In 1986 the Netherlands Institute for War Documentation performed a scientific study of the diary. They studied the ink and compared the handwriting in the different versions. They concluded that the diary is authentic and that Anne Frank wrote it during the war.

EDUCATION AND UNDERSTANDING

Along with becoming a best-selling book, Anne's diary was adapted into several different films and theater plays. Two film versions of the diary were released, one in 1959 and one in 1980. Both films won several awards. A play based on the book opened on Broadway in New York City in 1955. The show also performed in Germany and the Netherlands in 1956. In 1997 another version of

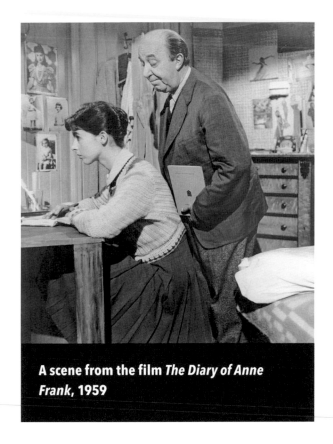

A scene from the film *The Diary of Anne Frank*, 1959

the play opened in New York City. Actor Natalie Portman played Anne.

While Otto Frank originally hesitated to publish his daughter's diary, he came to recognize the impact Anne's words could have. He believed the diary could educate people about the war and teach people to treat others with respect. He eventually stopped working for Opekta to concentrate on the diary. Many who read Anne's diary wrote letters to Frank, and he responded to these letters. In the early 1950s, he moved to Switzerland and married a woman who had also survived Auschwitz. In 1963 Frank opened the Anne Frank Foundation in

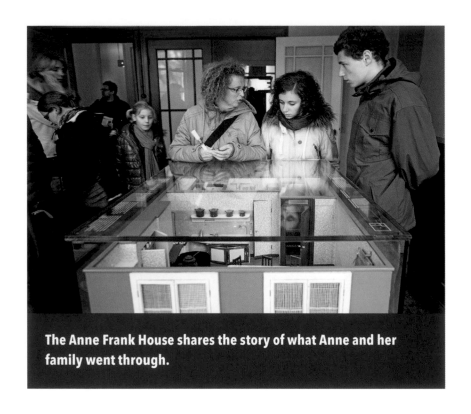

The Anne Frank House shares the story of what Anne and her family went through.

Basel, Switzerland. This foundation's goals are education, charity, and the fight against anti-Semitism. Upon his death in 1980, the foundation owned Anne's writings. It continues its work in education and charity.

Other organizations dedicated to Anne Frank's memory have opened as well. One Amsterdam organization runs the Anne Frank House, at 263 Prinsengracht, where Anne and the others hid. Visitors to the museum can see the rooms where Anne and the others lived for more than two years during the war. The magazine cutouts of movie stars are still pasted on the walls in Anne's room.

In 2017 the Anne Frank Foundation authorized a new version of Anne's diary. This version retells Anne's story as a graphic novel. The Anne Frank Foundation also plans to release a new film called *Where Is Anne Frank?* The film imagines Kitty becoming a real girl and trying to learn about the last seven months of Anne's life.

Since the diary's first publication in 1947, many young people around the world have read Anne's story. Anne was, in many ways, a typical teenager. The thoughts, dreams, and observations she wrote in her diary reflect the thoughts, dreams, and ideas of

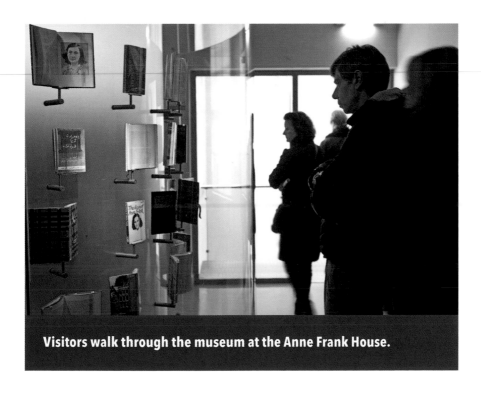

Visitors walk through the museum at the Anne Frank House.

young people generations later. Yet Anne was living in an extraordinary time. She suffered tremendous persecution and witnessed terrible things. Many of the young readers who encounter her story will never experience this kind of suffering. However, Anne's writing continues to teach its readers important lessons about tolerance and hope.

In the last entry Anne wrote in her diary, on August 1, 1944, she was frustrated with herself. She felt that two versions of herself were inside her. One was the funny, happy girl that others could see. The other, however, was quiet and serious. Anne wished she could show this part of herself more often. She felt that this was who she truly

A guest goes through the secret passageway at the Anne Frank House.

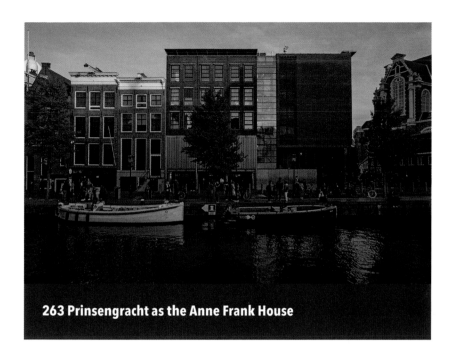

263 Prinsengracht as the Anne Frank House

was. Anne wrote that she felt she had to hide her true self and that she was afraid of what others might think if she let this side show. But despite her frustration and fear, she remained optimistic. She wrote that she had to "keep trying to find a way to become what I'd like to be and what I could be if . . . if only there were no other people in the world."

IMPORTANT DATES

June 12, 1929   Annelies Marie Frank is born in Frankfurt, Germany.

March 24, 1933   Adolf Hitler becomes a dictator in Germany.

Summer 1933   Otto Frank moves to Amsterdam, and his family follows a year later.

May 10, 1940   Germany invades the Netherlands.

June 12, 1942   Anne receives a diary for her thirteenth birthday.

July 6, 1942   The Frank family goes into hiding at 263 Prinsengracht.

July 13, 1942   The van Pels family moves into the hiding place with the Frank family.

November 16, 1942   Fritz Pfeffer moves into the hiding place.

August 4, 1944   All eight of those in hiding are discovered and sent to Westerbork.

September 3, 1944   The occupants of the hiding place are sent by train to Auschwitz.